As always...

**This book is dedicated
to all my friends,
supporters and readers,
and the love of my life.**

THANK YOU

VEGAN SAUCE
30+ Plant Based Diet Recipes
(vol. 5)

Tasty, Healthy, Amazing

by Vivian Green

The Tasty, Healthy, Amazing Collection:

Vegan Breakfast
30+ Plant Based Diet Recipes To Kickstart Your Day

Vegan Lunch
30+ Plant Based Diet Recipes To Keep You Satisfied

Vegan Dinner
30+ Plant Diet Based Recipes To Feel Great at The End of The Day

Vegan Dessert
30+ Plant Based Diet Recipes To Sweeten The Pot

Vegan Sauce
30+ Plant Based Diet Recipes To Spice Your Meals

Vegan Snack
30+ Plant Based Diet Recipes To Stay on Top

30+ Plant Based Diet Recipes

Table of Contents

INTRODUCTION... VEGAN SAUCES

It's a known culinary fact that a sauce can make or break any dish. Vegans are all about adding layers of flavor to food using various seasonings and sauces.

If you're in the market to dress up your meals with liquid flavor, stock your fridge and pantry with recurring essentials: tahini, nutritional yeast, miso, cocoa powder and cashews. These five ingredients are the bases of countless, dairy-free sauces and no law-abiding vegan can live without them.

As far as equipment goes, a blender and food processor (plus a few bowls for mixing) are key to making a sauce out of just about anything.

While the world of vegan sauces is vast, here are a couple common classics and some unique concoctions to get you started.

SALAD DRESSINGS

RASPBERRY VINAIGRETTE

This dressing is great for tying together a salad that has both veggie and fruity elements. The raspberries offer a tangy and sweet twist that's perfect for bringing some interest to simple green salads. Top it off with some toasted almonds to seal the deal.

Yield: about 2 cups

Ingredients:

1/2 cup (75 g) raspberries, fresh or frozen

1/4 cup (60 ml) apple cider vinegar

1/4 cup (60 ml) balsamic vinegar

2 teaspoons (10 g) sugar

1 tablespoon (15 g) dijon mustard

1/4 cup (60 ml) vegetable oil

Directions:

Combine all ingredients, except for oil, in the bowl of a blender and blend until smooth.

Slowly drizzle in the oil with the engine running until the dressing emulsifies.

Simple Cesar

Normally made with anchovies to give it an extra punch, this Cesar takes out the fish while preserving the bold flavor. You can pour it over classic romaine and croutons or get inventive and try it drizzled over a faux-chicken sandwich.

Yield: about 1/2 cup

Ingredients:

2 cloves garlic

1 tablespoon (15 ml) lemon juice

1 teaspoon (5 ml) vegetarian Worcestershire sauce

1 teaspoon (5 g) onion powder

1 teaspoon (5 g) Dijon mustard

1/2 cup (120 ml) olive oil

dash salt

Directions:

Place everything except for oil in the bowl of a food processor and blend until combined.

With the food processor running, drizzle in olive oil until the mixture is creamy.

MISO GINGER

The tang of miso and the complex flavor of ginger marry well in this dressing. A great topper to Asian-inspired salads, this dressing also contains digestive aiding properties due to ginger's ability to settle your grumbling belly.

Yield: about 1 cup

Ingredients:

1/4 cup (48 g) miso

2 tablespoons (30 ml) rice vinegar

2 tablespoons (30 ml) soy sauce

2 tablespoons (30 ml) sesame oil

1/2 teaspoon (3 g) minced fresh ginger

water as needed

Directions:

Add all ingredients to a medium mixing bowl and whisk to combine.

Add water a bit at a time and incorporate until you reach your desired consistency.

Blood Orange Vinaigrette

When you're in the mood for something fancier than OJ, blood orange steps in to give you a colorful variation on a super-citrusy vinaigrette that looks as good as it tastes. Give it an extra hit of antioxidants with a splash of pomegranate juice.

Yield: 4 servings

Ingredients:

1/2 cup (120 ml) red wine vinegar

1/3 cup (65 g) sugar

1/4 cup (60 ml) blood orange juice

2 teaspoons (10 g) dried mustard

dash salt and pepper, or to taste

Directions:

Add everything to a medium mixing bowl and whisk to combine.

Adjust salt and pepper to taste.

CILANTRO-LIME

If you're in the mood for Mexican but lack the tortillas to make tacos a reality, this dressing comes to the rescue. Just toss it with some spinach, avocado, black beans and corn to take yourself way south of the border without having to go to the market.

Yield: 1 1/2 cups

Ingredients:

1 jalapeno pepper, seeded and coarsely chopped

1 clove garlic

3/4 teaspoon (4 g) minced fresh ginger root

1/4 cup (60 ml) lime juice

1/3 cup (80 ml) light agave syrup

2 teaspoons (10 ml) balsamic vinegar

1/2 teaspoon (3 g) salt, or to taste

1/4 cup (22 g) packed cilantro leaves

1/2 cup (120 ml) extra-virgin olive oil

Directions:

Place all ingredients, except for olive oil in the bowl of a food processor and pulse until combined.

Turn food processor on and drizzle in olive oil until the dressing reaches your desired consistency.

Adjust salt and pepper to taste.

RAWISH RANCH

A creamy take on the dairy-full original, this dressing is thick and much like its traditional counterpart. Try dipping some carrot or celery sticks in this ranch or putting it out at parties to see if anyone notices a difference (they won't!)

Yield: about 3 cups

Ingredients:

1 1/2 cups (225 g) soaked cashews

3/4 to 1 (180-250 ml) cup water

2 cloves of garlic

1/4 cup (60 ml) olive oil

1/4 cup (60 ml) white rice vinegar

1 teaspoon (5 g) pepper

2 teaspoons (10 g) salt

1/2 teaspoon (3 ml) agave nectar

1 teaspoon (5 g) Italian herb seasoning

1 teaspoon (5 g) fresh dill, finely chopped

The juice of half a lemon

Directions:

Add cashews, 3/4 cup (180 ml) of water, garlic, olive oil, vinegar, agave, lemon, salt and pepper to the bowl of food process and blend until completely smooth. Add additional water if needed. Adjust salt and pepper to taste.

Transfer to the refrigerator to chill for a minimum of 2 hours.

Using a rubber spatula, mix in Italian seasoning and dill.

999 ISLAND

One island short of a thousand, this dressing tosses the cruelty but not the pickley flavor. Dress a simple salad for a decadent lunch or slather onto a burger to do something new at the BBQ.

Yield: about 4 servings

Ingredients:

1 cup (190 g) Vegenaise

1/3 cup (65 g) ketchup

1/2 teaspoon (3 g) onion powder

dash salt

3 tablespoons (30 g) sweet pickle relish

Directions:

Add all ingredients to a medium mixing bowl and stir together with a fork until well-combined.

LEMON POPPY SEED

For times when you've tossed the kitchen sink in your salad bowl, this dressing unifies random flavors without adding more confusion to the mix. A simple flavor profile, the sourness of the lemon juice freshens up any bowl of leftover veggies and the soaked cashews add a little creamy texture.

Yield: 1 1/2 cups

Ingredients:

1/2 cup (75 g) raw cashews, soaked for 30 minutes, rinsed in cold water

3/4 cup (180 ml) cold-pressed extra virgin olive oil

1/4 cup (60 ml) filtered water

3 tablespoons (45 ml) freshly squeezed lemon juice

2 tablespoons (30 ml) raw agave

1/2 teaspoon (3 g) fine sea salt

2 tablespoons (30 g) poppy seeds

Directions:

Blend everything, except for poppy seeds, in a food processor until no chunks remain.

Transfer to a small bowl and mix in poppy seeds by hand.

PASTA SAUCE (CREAMY)

QUESO SUPER FRESCO

Vegans are always on the hunt for cheese alternatives, and this recipe does the trick. This potato-based queso can turn a pound of plain pasta into a creamy alfredo in minutes. Don't stop at pasta; use this as a topping for nachos, dollop it on top of tacos or a put out as a dip for game time.

Yield: 2 cups

Ingredients:

1 cup (150 g) russet potato, peeled and chopped into 1" (2.5 cm) pieces

1 cup (150 g) cauliflower florets

1/3 cup (50 g) yellow onion, diced

1 cup (250 ml) water

1/4 cup (40 g) raw cashews

1 teaspoon (5 g) sea salt

1/4 teaspoon (2 g) minced garlic

1/4 teaspoon (2 g) Dijon mustard

1 tablespoon (15 ml) lemon juice

1/3 cup (65 g) Earth Balance margarine

Directions:

Bring water, potatoes, onions and cauliflower to a boil in a medium saucepan. Turn heat down to simmer, cover and cook for about 15 minutes or until you can pierce the potatoes with a fork. Allow to cool for 10 minutes. Drain and reserve cooking water.

Using a food processor, blend cashews, salt, garlic, mustard, lemon juice and margarine until smooth. Add vegetables and blend until smooth. Adjust the consistency to your liking by adding reserved cooking water, 1 tablespoon (15 ml) at a time. You can get it from a dip-like consistency to more of a sauce using this method.

CASHEW CHEESE

This is the grandfather recipe of how to make cheese from nuts. Soaking cashews gives them a creamy texture that acts as an excellent base that you can cheese-up with your preferred spices. Try rubbing this stuff into some kale for a cheesy side salad.

Yield: 1 1/2 cups

Ingredients:

1 cup (150 g) raw cashews

1/2 fresh red or yellow bell pepper, sliced

1/4 cup (60 ml) water

2 tablespoons (30 ml) fresh lemon juice

2 tablespoons (20 g) nutritional yeast

1 tablespoon (15 ml) tahini

1 1/2 teaspoons (7 g) sea salt

1 garlic clove

2 tsp. onion powder

Directions:

Place cashews in medium bowl and cover with water. Allow to soak for a minimum of two hours or overnight.

Drain cashews and place in the food processor with remaining ingredients.

Blend until smooth.

PROTEIN-PUNCH TOFU SAUCE

This sauce is nice and creamy with a big hit of protein from the whirled-in tofu. The texture works well with pasta, coating every strand in creamy goodness. Great for pouring on thick to make creamy mac and cheese, this sauce also works over broccoli and cauliflower. Herb it out with some parsley, basil or chives for a bit of green variation.

Yield: 8 servings

Ingredients:

2 pounds (1 kg) tofu, crumbled

8 cups (2 L) water

2 tablespoons (30 ml) tahini

2 tablespoons (30 ml) vegetable oil

2 tablespoons (30 ml) red wine vinegar

1 tablespoon (15 ml) soy sauce

2 teaspoons (10 g) dill, dried

2 teaspoons (10 ml) sesame oil

1 garlic clove, minced

Directions:

Blend all ingredients in a blender until smooth.

Adjust seasonings to taste.

Avocado Alfredo

This sauce is big on flavor and color. Aside from a beautiful presentation, using avocado creates a very rich and decadent sauce that pairs well with simple pasta dishes. The lemon and basil give it a fresh, bright flavor that tastes like a cross between pesto and guacamole.

Yield: 2 servings

Ingredients:

1 garlic clove, chopped

juice from 1/2 lemon

1 tablespoon (15 ml) olive oil

1/2 avocado, chopped

1/4 cup (15 g) basil leaves, chopped

dash of salt

Directions:

Blend garlic, lemon juice and olive oil in a food processor until combined.

Add avocado, basil and salt to processor and blend until smooth.

Pumpkin Sage

When pumpkin season is in full swing and everyone is craving that sweet, orange gourd, this sauce captures the essence of autumn. Sage has somewhat of a medicinal taste but pairs well with the creamy, squashy flavor of pumpkin. Finish off your pasta dish with a few toasted pumpkin seeds to round out the flavor profile.

Yield: 3 cups

Ingredients:

3 cloves minced garlic

1/2 diced onion

2 tablespoons (30 ml) olive oil

1 cup (250 ml) broth

3/4 cup (180 ml) soy milk

1 1/2 cups (225 g) canned or precooked pumpkin

1 teaspoon (5 g) sage

salt and pepper to taste

1/3 cup (50 g) finely chopped walnuts or pine nuts

Directions:

In a medium saucepan, saute onion and garlic in olive oil for about 3-5 minutes or until fragrant.

Turn the heat down to low and add pumpkin, vegetable broth, milk and sage. Simmer for 8-10 minutes, stirring occasionally.

Add salt, pepper, nuts and stir to combine.

Remove from heat and cool slightly before using.

PASTA SAUCE (NOT CREAMY)

PUTTANESCA

A classic Italian sauce that combines seemingly too salty components to create a sauce with just the right amount of tang to make your mouth water. Use a short pasta, like farfalle, penne or anything with deep ridges, to create a dish with the perfect pasta to mouth-watering sauce ratio.

Yield: 4 servings

Ingredients:

1 14.5 oz can diced tomatoes

1 teaspoon garlic, minced

1 tablespoon onion, minced

1 teaspoon olive oil

10 sliced green olives (any variety)

10 sliced black olives (any variety)

2 tablespoons (20 g) capers

1/4 - 1 teaspoon (2-5 g) red pepper flakes

salt and pepper to taste

Directions:

In a medium saucepan, saute onions and garlic for 3 minutes or until fragrant.

Stir in tomatoes, olives, capers and pepper flakes.

Reduce heat to simmer and cook for about 5 minutes,

Season with salt and pepper to taste.

CLASSIC TOMATO

Sometimes a plain, clean sauce served over al dente pasta makes for the best meals. This sauce has no fancy frills and is simple to prepare and the end result is a great way to highlight the quality of your ingredients.

Yield: 4 cups

Ingredients:

20 roma tomatoes, halved and seeded

1/4 cup (60 ml) olive oil

1/2 teaspoon (3 g) kosher salt

1 teaspoon (5 g) pepper

1 cup (150 g) finely diced onion

2 teaspoons (10 g) minced garlic

1 tablespoon (20 g) finely chopped oregano leaves

1 tablespoon (20 g) finely chopped thyme leaves

1 cup (250 ml) white wine

Directions:

Heat your oven to 325 degrees F (160 degrees C).

Place tomatoes cut side up on a large baking pan and drizzle with olive oil. Sprinkle with salt and pepper. Bake for 1 1/2 hours.

Crank the heat up to 400 degrees F (200 degrees C) and bake for another 30 minutes.

In a blender, combine tomatoes, garlic, oregano and thyme.

In a large saucepan, saute garlic on medium heat for 3 minutes.

Add wine and cook for 3 minutes.

Add tomato mixture and simmer on low for 8-10 minutes or until the mixture has reduced by about 25%.

MEATLESS MEATY MEAT SAUCE

Tempeh is a fantastic vegan protein that gives this sauce a meaty bite. It absorbs flavors well and creates a hearty sauce that can be jazzed up with a little vegan cheese for a filling dinner dish.

Yield: 8 servings

Ingredients:

2, 14.5 ounce (815 g) cans stewed tomatoes

1 small onion, peeled and halved

2 tablespoons (20 g) garlic, minced

1/8 teaspoon (1 g) red pepper flakes, crushed

1/2 teaspoon (3 g) oregano, dried

1/4 teaspoon (2 g) Kosher salt

1 tablespoon (15 ml) extra virgin olive oil

1 package tempeh, 3 grain, crumbled

Directions:

In a medium saucepan over medium heat, saute garlic in olive oil for 3 minutes or until fragrant.

Add tomatoes and mash a bit with your spatula until they are broken up, but still chunky.

Stir in the rest of the ingredients, except for tempeh.

Turn heat down to low and simmer, uncovered, for 10 minutes.

Remove onion halves and stir in tempeh.

Continue cooking for another 5 minutes.

BROWN BUTTER

This sauce is super versatile but has traditionally made appearances in gnocchi dishes paired with sage or another distinctly-flavored herb. Don't limit yourself though. You can toss regular old spaghetti in this stuff for a quick, gourmet-tasting dish.

Yield: 2 servings

Ingredients:

3 tablespoons (45 g) Earth Balance

2 teaspoons (10 g) chopped sage

1 teaspoon (5 g) chopped thyme

pinch of pepper flakes

1 pinch brown sugar

1 teaspoon (5 ml) balsamic vinegar

small pinch of salt to taste

Directions:

Add all ingredients to a medium skillet and bring to a low simmer on low heat (about 3-5 minutes).

At this point, toss whatever you want to coat in the sauce into the pan to coat.

Serve warm.

TOFU TOPPERS

Classic Basil Pesto

This sauce is a great way to use up that huge bunch of basil you bought. Packed with that fresh, herb-heavy taste, the pine nuts in this sauce really give it a nutty body that makes it delicious as both a spaghetti sauce and a protein topper.

Yields: 16 servings

Ingredients:

1/3 cup (50 g) pine nuts

2/3 cup (160 ml) olive oil

5 cloves garlic

1/3 cup (20 g) nutritional yeast

1 bunch fresh basil leaves

salt and pepper to taste

Directions:

Lightly toast pine nuts in a skillet.

Add pine nuts and remaining ingredients into food processor and blend until smooth.

Adjust salt and pepper to taste.

CRANBERRY PISTACHIO SAUCE

This pesto-like sauce is tart, tangy and colorful. Make sure you toast the pistachios before blending them in to give it an extra bit of complexity.

Yield: 6-8 servings

Ingredients:

1 cup (150 g) raw shelled pistachios

1/2 cup (75 g) dried cranberries, reconstituted

2 cloves garlic

1/2 cup (120 ml) olive oil

1/2 teaspoon (3 g) salt

1 teaspoon (5 g) whole coriander seeds

zest one lime

juice from one lime

Directions:

Rehydrate cranberries slightly by placing them in a bowl with a little water and microwaving on high for 2 minutes.

Drain cranberries and add them to the bowl of a food processor along with the remaining ingredients.

Process until a pesto consistency forms.

SUPER HOT JALAPENO

Wake up your palette with a hit of hot. The heat of jalapenos lives in their seeds so if you'd prefer a less spicy sauce, carefully remove all of the seeds and wash the knife before dicing them. If you're a heat freak and want something a little spicier, try using habaneros and burn a a hole in your gut.

Yield: 4 servings

Ingredients:

1/2 cup (120 ml) lemon juice

1-3 tablespoons (15-45 ml) grape seed oil

1 1/2 cups (225 g) raw walnuts

1 cup (150 g) pistachios, roasted/salted

3 tablespoons (45 ml) pasta water

1 small orange, squeezed

2 cups (180 g) fresh basil

1 small onion

1 jalapeno

5-8 cloves garlic

1 cup (90 g) fresh parsley

1 teaspoon (5 g) salt

1 teaspoon (5 g) pepper

Directions:

Throw everything in a food processor and blend until smooth and thick.

MUSHROOM GRAVY

Earthy and comforting, nothing says "home cooking" like gravy. Pour it on thick over tofu and mashed potatoes. Drizzle it on roasted root vegetables and add moisture to faux-meat sandwiches. Cremini mushrooms are a great, commonly-found mushroom to use but feel free to substitute whatever variety you have on hand (or a combination of various mushrooms works even better).

Yield: 8-10 servings

Ingredients:

4 cups (1 L) vegetable broth
1/2 cup (60 g) all purpose flour
1 medium yellow onion, diced small
2 tablespoons (30 ml) olive oil
16 ounces (450 g) cremini mushrooms, thinly sliced and chopped
4 cloves garlic, minced
2 teaspoons (10 g) dried thyme
1 teaspoon (5 g) dried sage
1/2 teaspoon (3 g) salt
Several dashes fresh black pepper
1/2 cup (120 ml) dry white wine, like chardonnay
2 tablespoons (10 g) nutritional yeast

Directions:

Combine flour and 2 cups (500 ml) of vegetable broth in a bowl. Mix until fully combined then add the remaining vegetable broth and set aside.

In a medium pot, saute onions in olive oil until translucent or about 5 minutes. Stir in mushrooms, garlic, thyme, sage, salt and pepper and continue to cook for another 5 minutes or until vegetable soften.

Deglaze with wine and turn the heat up to high. Bring mixture to a boil and allow wine to reduce by cooking for another 3 minutes.

Stir in broth mixture and nutritional yeast. Turn heat down to medium and cook until the gravy thickens, for about 20 minutes, stirring frequently.

Adjust salt and pepper to taste.

CHIPOTLE ENCHILADA SAUCE

A Mexican flavor explosion, don't limit yourself to just slathering enchiladas in this smokey sauce. Try it on a simply-spiced grilled tofu steak (salt, pepper, maybe a little cumin) with a few Mexican sides like black beans and corn.

Yield: 2-3 servings

Ingredients:

1/2 onion, chopped
1 clove garlic, minced
1 tablespoon (15 g) chili powder
1-2 teaspoons (5-10 g) chipotle chili powder
1/2 teaspoon (3 g) oregano
1/2 teaspoon (3 g) cumin
1, 14 ounce (400 g) can crushed roasted tomatoes
3/4 cup (180 ml) water
1 teaspoon (5 g) brown sugar
salt and pepper to taste

Directions:

In a medium sauce pan over medium heat, saute onions and garlic in olive oil until fragrant or about 5 minutes.

Stir in spices and continue cooking for 2 minutes.

Deglaze with water and stir in tomatoes.

Turn heat up to high and bring mixture to a boil.

Once boiling, turn heat down to low and simmer for 20 minutes.

Adjust salt and pepper to taste.

MANGO CHUTNEY

Chutneys are the perfect blend of spicy, salty and sweet. This chunky sauce originates from India and while mango variety has become the most popular, using sweet, ripe peaches makes a great variation on this recipe as well.

Yield: 2/3 cup

Ingredients:

1 teaspoon (5 ml) coconut oil

1 diced champagne mango

1/2 inch (13 mm) ginger grated

1/2 teaspoon (3 g) red chili flakes

1 clove garlic chopped

1/4 teaspoon (2 g) salt

2 tablespoons (30 ml) cider vinegar

2 tablespoons (30 ml) packed brown sugar

2 tablespoons (20 g) golden raisins

1/8 teaspoon (1 g) each of ground cinnamon, clove, cardamom, nutmeg

Directions:

Heat oil in a large pot on medium heat.

Throw in all of the ingredients and stir to combine.

Turn heat down to medium-low and bring mixture to a rolling boil.

Reduce heat to low and simmer for 25 minutes, stirring often.

Adjust spices to taste.

REFRESHING CUCUMBER SAUCE

If the rest of your meal is a bit spicy, topping your protein with this cooling sauce makes for a well-balanced dish. A great summer sauce, toss it with some radishes for an extra chill side dish.

Yield: 6 servings

Ingredients:

1 cup (190 g) soy yogurt, unsweetened

12 small cucumbers, peeled and grated

1 tablespoon (15 ml) fresh lemon juice

1 tablespoon (7 g) dill weed, dried

1-2 tablespoons (15-30 g) salt

Directions:

Using a box grater, grate cucumber into a colander and set in the sink to drain for about 10 minutes.

Remove remaining water from the cucumber by squeezing gently. Transfer cucumber to a small bowl.

Stir in remaining ingredients, cover and set in the refrigeration for at least 1 hour before serving.

Spicy Peanut Sauce

Great for Thai-inspired dishes, this sauce can be used for dipping, as well as a drizzling. Try serving it alongside tofu or seitan skewers or as a compliment to vegetable spring rolls.

Yield: 4-5 servings

Ingredients:

2/3 cup (160 g) peanut butter

1/4 cup (60 ml) soy sauce

3 cloves garlic, minced

2 green onions, diced

2 tablespoons (30 ml) sesame oil

1/2 teaspoon (3 g) powdered ginger

1/2 teaspoon (3 g) cayenne pepper

juice from 2 limes

2 tablespoons (20 g) sesame seeds

Directions:

Add all ingredients to a sauce pan and heat on low, stirring often, until peanut butter melts and everything is well-combined (3-4 minutes).

Remove from heat and serve.

RED HOT CURRY

Simmering your protein in this sauce creates a complexity of flavors unmatched by anything you can pour on top. Thai basil is used here and it differs from traditional Italian basil in that its a bit sweeter. This sauce requires a little bit of patience but develops a lot of depth with time.

Yield: 4 servings

Ingredients:

5 dried red chillies

8 cloves garlic peeled

1 medium sized onion-roughly chopped

1/4 cup (22 g) tightly packed basil leaves

1/4 cup (60 ml) full fat coconut milk

1 pound (450 g) fresh mushrooms, roughly chopped

2 green peppers-chopped roughly

1/2 cup (75 g) frozen peas.

2 tablespoons (24 g) tomato puree

Salt

pinch turmeric

1 tablespoon (15 ml) peanut oil / vegetable oil

Directions:

Combine water, garlic, onion and chillies in a medium sauce pan set over high heat. Bring to a boil then turn down heat to low and simmer until vegetable soften, about 8 minutes.

Transfer to a bowl and allow to cool. Reserve boiling water.

Add garlic, onion, chillies, basil and about 1 tablespoon of boiling water to a food processor and process into a paste. Set aside.

In a medium sauce span, heat oil for 2 minutes on medium heat. Stir in green peppers, turmeric and salt. Cook for 3-4 minutes or until fragrant.

Stir in mushrooms and peas and continue cooking for 5 minutes or until vegetables are just about fully-cooked.

Stir in the paste you made, tomato puree, coconut milk and salt to taste.

Remove from heat and serve garnished with a bit of chopped fresh basil.

KIWI WITH A KICK

Kiwi fruit is underutilized in the culinary world. Here, it takes center stage as a mouth-watering, fruity sauce that creates a beautiful green presentation. If you're looking to impress someone with sauce, this should be your go-to recipe. Simple to prepare, and delicious to devour, this sauce is fantastic on anything from mock duck to uncooked (but drained and pressed) tofu slabs.

Yield: 4 servings

Ingredients:

2 ripe kiwis, pealed and pureed

2 ounces (48 g) agave syrup

juice of 1/2 lemon

1 teaspoon (5 g) mint, chopped

pinch cayenne pepper

3 tablespoons (45 ml) soy sauce

freshly ground black pepper to taste

Directions:

Stir all ingredients together in a small bowl until well-combined.

Refrigerate until ready to use.

DESSERT DRIZZLES

Chocolate Ganache

Putting rich, creamy chocolate on just about anything makes for a great dish. This is a basic recipe for ganache that you can use to spread like frosting on top of cakes, pastries and fruit, for a touch of fancy pants. Eat it by the spoonful or bake it into molten lava cake. Whichever method of consumption you choose, this is a dessert sauce that will always satisfy your sweet tooth.

Yield: 8 servings

Ingredients:

3/4 cup (180 ml) unsweetened almond milk
6 ounces(170 g) 72% dark chocolate
3 tablespoons (45 ml) maple syrup
1/4 cup (25 g) confectioner's sugar, sifted

Directions:

Add all ingredients to a small pot and heat on low, stirring often, until chocolate is melted and mixture is fully combined.

Remove from heat and refrigerate if you want a thicker consistency.

BLACKBERRY

A deep, luscious berry sauce with great seedy texture. Try it as a topper to any peach dessert like cobbler or simple grilled peaches. Set aside a few whole berries to garnish for a beautiful presentation.

Yield: 2 cups

Ingredients:

3/4 cup (180 ml) water

1/2 cup (100 g) raw sugar

1 inch (13 mm) piece vanilla bean, halved

1 cup (150 g) blackberries

Directions:

Add sugar and water to a medium saucepan over medium heat. Scrape the seeds of the vanilla bean into the mixture and throw in the bean itself.

Bring to a simmer and allow to cook for about 10 minutes, stirring frequently.

Turn up heat to medium-high and bring mixture to a boil.

Remove the vanilla bean and add the blackberries.

Cook for 10 minutes, stirring occasionally, until the blackberries start to break down.

Remove from heat, cool for 5 minutes and transfer to a food processor. Blend until smooth.

CARAMEL

Traditional caramel is basically made with just a ton of sugar and butter. No dairy is necessary to get that browned buttery flavor and this basic recipe shows you how to best veganize the classic. Let this caramel inspire your next ice cream sundae.

Yield: 1 1/2 cups

Ingredients:

1 cup (200 g) cane sugar
1/4 cup (60 ml) water
1 teaspoon (5 ml) vanilla extract
3 tablespoons (45 g) Earth Balance
3 to 4 tablespoons (45-60 ml) almond milk

Directions:

Set an 8 inch (20 cm) cake pan in the freezer.

Warm up a large, heavy-bottomed skillet over medium-high heat.

Add sugar and stir constantly with a wooden spoon until it melts.

Add 1/4 cup (60 ml) of water and continue stirring for 2-3 minutes until the sugar begins to caramelize.

Incorporate vanilla and allow sugar to darken a bit.

Stir in Earth Balance and continue stirring for another 2-3 minutes or until Earth Balance is fully incorporated and the mixture begins to boil.

Add almond milk one tablespoon (15 ml) at a time until you reach your desired creaminess and cook for another 4 minutes. Remove from heat and allow to rest for 1 minute.

Transfer mixture to cold cake pan and allow to cool for 20 minutes before using.

BUTTERSCOTCH

With the word "butter" right there in your face, you'd think this sauce would be completely off-limits to vegans. Well, you'd be totally wrong. With new developments in vegan butter replacements (like Earth Balance), butterscotch can be made completely vegan (and totally delicious).

Yield: 1/2-3/4 cup

Ingredients:

3/4 cup (135 g) brown sugar

3 tablespoons (45 ml) water

3 tablespoons (45 g) Earth Balance

3 tablespoons (45 ml) corn syrup

scant 1/8 teaspoon (1 g) salt

Directions:

Attach a candy thermometer to the side of a heavy-bottomed sauce pan and add all of your ingredients to the pan.

Over medium-high heat, stir until the sugar begins to melt.

Allow the mixture to bubble until the thermometer indicates 240 degrees F.

Quickly remove from heat.

Allow to cool for 20 minutes then transfer to a glass container with a lid (like a mason jar) for storage.

CHERRY

At the peak of summer, this jammy sauce is a great way to preserve your cherry bounty. A great filling for vegan danishes, as a spread on toast or a crepe-topper, this sauce is tart, sweet and a perfect way to end a nice summer dinner.

Yield: about 2 cups

Ingredients:

1/2 cup (100 g) sugar

Juice and zest of 1 lemon

2 cups (300 g) frozen, pitted cherries

1 tablespoon (15 g) Cornstarch

Directions:

Add all ingredients to a small saucepan over medium heat.

Cook until sugar melts (stir often) and sauce takes on a thick consistency (about 10 minutes).

THANKS!

Thanks to all readers and now vegan cooks who took the time to put these recipes into action. The Tasty, Healthy, Amazing recipes collection is starting to become quite big. So as usual at the end of each of these Vegan recipes cookbooks, here's a BIG THANK YOU for your support.

This book certainly has the quickest recipes of the collection, so get these sauces done and your meals will taste even better.

We will soon meet again, as I have few more things to tell you. I hope you enjoyed my recipes so far and will forever be grateful to have readers who have been with me all the way.

     Vivian ;)

The Tasty, Healthy, Amazing Collection:

Vegan Breakfast
30+ Plant Based Diet Recipes To Kickstart Your Day

Vegan Lunch
30+ Plant Based Diet Recipes To Keep You Satisfied

Vegan Dinner
30+ Plant Diet Based Recipes To Feel Great at The End of The Day

Vegan Dessert
30+ Plant Based Diet Recipes To Sweeten The Pot

Vegan Sauce
30+ Plant Based Diet Recipes To Spice Your Meals

Vegan Snack
30+ Plant Based Diet Recipes To Stay on Top

30+ Plant Based Diet Recipes

Made in the USA
Las Vegas, NV
24 October 2023